Fred Gwynne

A Chocolate Moose

for Dinner

written and illustrated by
FRED GWYNNE

Windmill Books and E. P. Dutton & Co., Inc. New York

First published, 1976, in the United States
by Windmill Books, Inc. & E. P. Dutton & Co., Inc.,
201 Park Avenue South, New York, New York 10003.
All rights reserved under International
and Pan-American Copyright Conventions.

LIBRARY OF CONGRESS CATALOGING IN PUBLICATION DATA

Gwynne, Fred. A chocolate moose for dinner

SUMMARY: A little girl pictures the things her parents
talk about, such as a chocolate moose, a gorilla war, and
shoe trees.

[1. English language—Homonyms—Fiction]   I.   Title
PZ7.G99Ch   [Fic]   76-4811

ISBN: 0-525-61545-8 (cloth)   ISBN: 0-525-62317-5 (paper)

Published simultaneously in Canada by Clarke,
Irwin & Company, Limited, Toronto and Vancouver

Designed by Dorothea von Elbe
Printed and bound in Japan by Dai Nippon Co., Ltd., Tokyo.

First Edition 10   9   8   7   6   5   4   3   2   1

For Keiron, Gaynor, Madyn, Evan, and Furlaud

**Mommy says
she had a
chocolate moose
for dinner last night.**

And after dinner

she toasted Daddy.

there's a gorilla war.

Daddy says
he has trees
for all his shoes.

Daddy says lions pray on

other  animals.

Daddy says he hates

the arms race.

Daddy says there should

Mommy says her

favorite painter is Dolly.

Mommy says there are airplane hangers.

Daddy says he has the best fishing tackle.

He spent two years in the pen.

And he has just escaped and is now on the lamb.

At the ocean Daddy says

watch out for the under toe.

Daddy says he plays the piano by ear.

Daddy says that in college

people row in shells.

And some row
in a single skull.

Mommy says after she and Daddy argue they always kiss and make up.

**Mommy says
she's going to tell me
about Santa Claws.**

And Daddy says he's going to tell me the story of

the tortoise and  the hair.

Stories
like these
drive me
up a wall!